The Last Days of Stonewall Jackson

BY RALPH HAPPEL

EASTERN NATIONAL • FORT WASHINGTON, PENNSYLVANIA

Cover illustration of Stonewall Jackson reproduced from the collections of the Library of Congress. Unless explicitly stated all photographs and images courtesy of Fredericksburg and Spotsylvania County Battlefields National Military Park.

Published by Eastern National in cooperation with Fredericksburg and Spotsylvania County Battlefields National Military Park.

© Eastern National, 2003.
Fort Washington, Pennsylvania 19034
Reprinted—1976, 1988, 1992, 2003
All rights reserved. Second edition.
ISBN 1-59091-006-0

Library of Congress Cataloging-in-Publication Data

Happel, Ralph.
 The last days of Stonewall Jackson / by Ralph Happel.— 2nd ed.
    p. cm.
 Rev. ed. of: Jackson.
 ISBN 1-59091-006-0 (pbk.)
 1. Jackson, Stonewall, 1824-1863. 2. Generals—Confederate States of America—Biography. 3. Confederate States of America. Army—Biography. 4. United States—History—Civil War, 1861-1865—Campaigns. I. Happel, Ralph. Jackson. II. Title.
  E467.1.J15H25 2003
  973.7'3'092--dc21

2003007760

Contents

Foreword	9
Two Interludes	11
A Volley in the Dark	17
Destination Fairfield	27
Over the River	35
A Busy Depot	47
Fairfield: Decay and Restoration	55
Acknowledgements	63

Let us cross over the river . . .

. . . and rest under the shade of the trees.

Foreword

Few persons know more about the military operations around Fredericksburg than did Ralph Happel. Few persons are better able to blend social history with military history; few know more about Jackson—the man and the general; and none are more generous, more willing to share knowledge of a particular subject.

Mr. Happel shared his enthusiasm with me twenty-four years ago; it was an incident I am sure he forgot the day after it happened. A young soldier stationed at a military post, I arrived as a visitor at Fredericksburg on a cold winter's day. True, there were no other visitors about; still, Mr. Happel could have answered my questions briefly and sent me on my way. But he didn't. The conversation stretched out for hours and ran from military operations to the personalities involved, the effect of social and economic conditions on the fighting, interaction and sometimes conflicts between troops from different states serving on the same side, and a host of other things.

A loyal native son of the Commonwealth of Virginia, Mr. Happel was a graduate of Mr. Jefferson's university—the University of Virginia. From that institution he received his bachelor's degree in 1932 and his master's in 1934. He started his career in the National Park Service as a research worker and guide in 1936. He served as an historian at Fredericksburg, Appomattox Court House, and Petersburg. In this narrative, Mr. Happel does not just recount history—he puts warm, living flesh on what might simply be the cold, dry, bare bones of historical narrative. Though he yields to no one in respect for Jackson as a man and a soldier, he is always concerned with the human condition rather than hero worship. I hope other readers enjoy this account as much as I have.

William K. Kay

Two Interludes

Standing in the rain at Guinea's Station, twelve miles down the railroad from war-torn Fredericksburg, a tense figure, ramrod straight, enveloped in his raincoat and his dreams, awaited the Richmond express train. On the cars would be his wife and baby.

Lieutenant General Thomas Jonathan ("Stonewall") Jackson, Confederate States Army, on this wet twentieth of April, 1863 had not yet seen Julia, his third child. The first was stillborn and the mother, Elinor Junkin, died by its birth. The devout Jackson married another Presbyterian minister's daughter, Mary Anna Morrison, in 1857. Their first infant survived but a few weeks. R. E. Lee's awesome lieutenant had then been an obscure professor of Natural Philosophy at the Virginia Military Institute in Lexington. He also taught Artillery Tactics and served as the butt of cadet jokes, "Old Jack," stiff and awkward. When the Civil War erupted and he was up for a command, a Virginia legislator inquired, "Who is this Major Jackson?" Everybody soon knew what he became, an American Cromwell striding mountain and valley, but still awkward.

Some said he was crazy. He did, indeed, seem to have his share of eccentricities. This dyspeptic teetotaler who used no tobacco was secretive, a point of military wisdom lost on many of his contemporaries. He absentmindedly sucked lemons, which, whatever the impression created, combatted the risk of scurvy common to hard rations. He held his hand up in the air on the march and in battle (like a centurion saluting Caesar) and the habit may well have eased tension. (It also got him shot in the finger at Manassas.) And he prayed any old time, which, whether or not it affected the course of events, eased his soul; he confided in God rather than man. He avoided posting or reading letters on Sunday, but he cheerfully engaged the enemy that day if the die so fell. (Not all of his habits were generally known. The army was unaware of his therapy of dousing his head in a basin of cold water to bathe his eyes.)

His martial capabilities, founded on West Point training, experience in the Mexican War and years of discipline, flowered in the Shenandoah Valley and at Second Manassas. Most recently, in December of 1862, he and his stalwart fellow corps commander James Longstreet had handily repulsed Ambrose Burnside's Federals at Fredericksburg. Though ever alert and mindful of war, Jackson, like his commander Robert E. Lee, did not glory in it. His private thoughts were of home. Spring having dried the roads, Burnside's successor Joseph Hooker might start something any day, if Lee did not move first. So Anna Jackson and the baby must hurry before a new campaign began to roll across the greening countryside.

Waiting at Guinea's Station, Jackson the family man looked forward to an interlude of domestic tranquility, his blue-gray eyes, so cold on occasion, warm with anticipation. At last came the sound of iron wheel rumbling on iron track, then the piercing whistle, and now here was the engine hissing to a stop! Loping up, the eternal farm boy pushed into his wife's car and flashed the domestic smile which the world seldom saw. The baby beamed back. It was love at first sight for both of them.

He bundled his little family and the child's nurse Hetty (who had been Anna's nurse) into a waiting carriage, and they set off for the Yerby house, Belvoir, at the southern end of the Fredericksburg battlefield, where his corps was gathered, ready for action.

Just past Guinea's Station, another plantation house stood on its rise overlooking the railroad, Thomas Coleman Chandler's Fairfield, a brick dwelling with a frame outbuilding in the yard. If the Yerbys were good to Jackson now, the Chandlers had been equally so last

December when his corps had camped briefly in the Guinea area and his tent had been pitched on Fairfield land. The Chandlers had refused to let Jackson's shyness daunt them. Mr. Chandler and his daughter Lucy went over to invite the General to set up headquarters in the parlor of the big house, out of the cold and damp. The General declined politely, stating he "never wished to fare better than his soldiers."

At least, thought the Chandlers, they would make sure that "Stonewall," hard as the nickname he acquired at First Manassas, would get some decent cooking. The Chandler servants, however, were sent back with the untasted meals and Jackson's thanks; he would let them know if he needed anything. His own servant Jim Lewis admitted to Mrs. Chandler that the General was "mighty peculiar."

Jackson finally broke down, though he would not shift headquarters. To his wife he reported, ". . . Wherever I go, God gives me kind friends. The people here show me great kindness . . . and a great many provisions are sent me, including nice cakes, tea, loaf-sugar, etc., and the socks and gloves and handkerchiefs still come!"

"Should I remain here," he wrote in the same letter, "I do hope you and baby can come to see me before spring, as you can come on the railroad."

He had not remained there; the peaceful Fairfield interlude lasted only a brief time, but, just the same, here were wife and baby ultimately arrived at Guinea's Station.

All the way to Thomas Yerby's, Jackson remarked on Julia's size and beauty. In his wet clothing he was afraid to pick her up. Inside the Yerby house, he tore off rain gear and gathered her in his arms. The spacious mansion could hardly contain his happiness.

The Jacksons were given the room recently occupied by General Lee during a severe illness. Lee himself soon rode over to make Anna welcome. The Yerby household and staff officers vied in attentions to "Stonewall's" modest *esposita* (little wife), as her husband called her in the Spanish he acquired during the Mexican War. Every moment to be

Monument marking Jackson's fall, dedicated 1888.

spared from duty Jackson spent at Belvoir, where the baby was rarely out of his arms. If she was asleep, he knelt in admiration over the cradle. This pride was almost too worldly for Deacon Jackson of the Lexington Presbyterian Church.

Pride aside, religion and family life happily coincided. On April 23, Julia was five months old. A distinguished Presbyterian divine who preached at Jackson's headquarters, the Reverend Beverley Tucker

Lacy, baptized her in the Yerby parlor in the presence of family and staff, including Jackson's two aides: Anna's brother Joseph and James Power Smith, a ministerial student before the war. The next Sunday the Jacksons attended open-air services with Lee and a large group of officers and soldiers. Mrs. Jackson thought Lacy's earnest message was edifying, and the grand volume of song impressed her. His family with him and his men praising the Lord, Jackson was content. Short of a successful peace and a return to home and garden, he could ask for no greater felicity on this earth.

Restraint seemed to fall from the General like the old coat discarded in favor of the handsome uniform presented to him by the cavalryman J. E. B. Stuart. Thomas Jackson bragged of his baby ("isn't she a *little gem?*"); he showed off for his wife on his spirited bay Superior (saving the dependable campaigner Little Sorrel for more serious work); and he acted altogether like a gay Cavalier rather than the Puritan he was presumed to be. He even agreed to go through with the chore of having his likeness taken again. A photographer, up from Richmond, posed him in the Yerby hallway. Anna arranged his curly brown hair, which was longer than he usually wore it. He turned military in the end, however, perhaps because a wind through the open hall made him frown, and the profile portrait afterwards so admired by his soldiers never greatly pleased his wife. She preferred a photograph taken earlier in the war at Winchester; that full-faced likeness pictured "the beaming sunlight of his *home-look*."

On the morning of the 29th of April word came that the Federals were beginning to act up. Thomas gave Anna a tender goodby, and General Jackson left Yerby's without breakfast. Soon the roar of cannon rattled the Belvoir windows. Joseph Morrison felt he should stay with the staff; so Chaplain Lacy escorted Anna, baby and nurse to Guinea's Station. Back to Richmond went the little family, leaving T. J. Jackson and his Second Corps of Lee's Army of Northern Virginia to prepare for battle.

A Volley in the Dark

General Hooker, whose bragging troubled President Lincoln, nevertheless initiated a fine plan of campaign. Joe Hooker would not make Burnside's mistake of attacking Lee's well-nigh impregnable concentration on the Fredericksburg hills. He would threaten that area, yes, leaving the dependable John Sedgwick's command for the purpose, but he would rely on a turning column moving up the Rappahannock (which bends westward above Fredericksburg) to cross and come in on Lee's rear. The Rappahannock, tidal to Fredericksburg, widens and deepens below the town; upstream, however, it becomes a narrow inland river.

When Sedgwick threw pontoons across the river below Fredericksburg and began skirmishing with Jackson's Corps on April 29, Hooker's turning force was well along in its march upcountry. The Confederates held fortifications at Banks' Ford, five miles up, and U.S. Ford, ten miles up, just below the junction of the Rappahannock and the Rapidan. Hooker's column went right past those fords to Kelly's, twenty-five miles from Fredericksburg. There the Federals crossed the Rappahannock and turned east. Next, they had the Rapidan to cross. Though road networks made fords and destroyed bridge sites practicable points for passage of an army, large bodies of infantry rarely forded even shallow rivers. Pontoon bridges were vital, especially during the high water of spring. After marching over the pontoons at Kelly's, however, the Union vanguard pushed on to wade the swirling Rapidan, waist-deep at Germanna and Ely's fords.

During April 30, the columns reached a crossroads ten miles west of Fredericksburg, where stood Chancellorsville, not a town, but a large brick house, formerly a tavern, then occupied by women and children, family

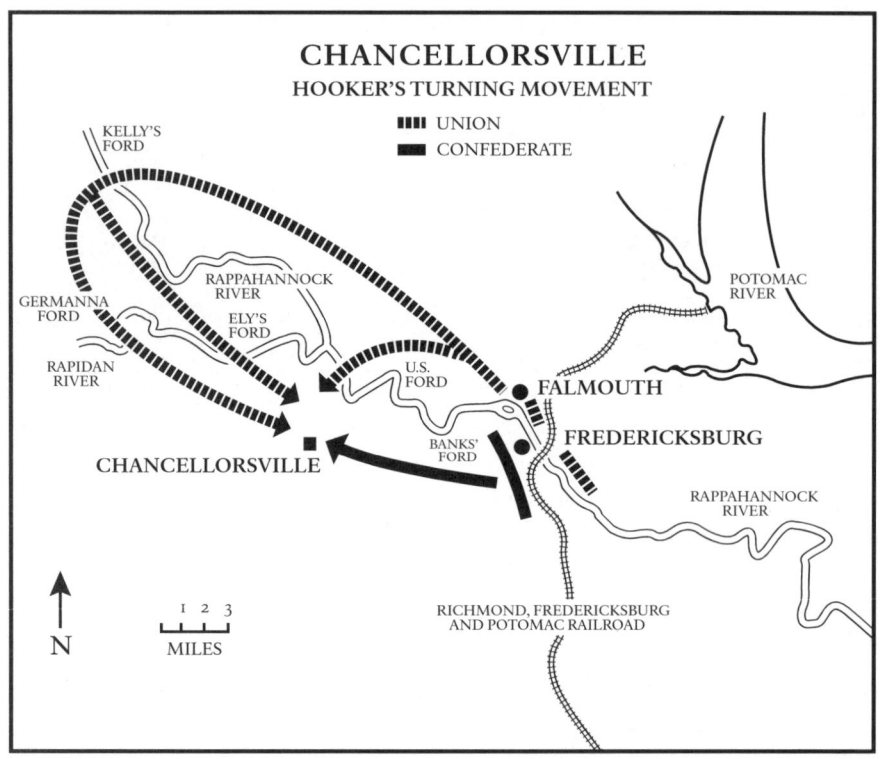

and refugees. Here converged the routes from the fords and the roads to Fredericksburg. U.S. Ford, taken in rear, served as the crossing place for Hooker's reinforcements. Hooker himself crossed at U.S. Ford and set up headquarters in the Chancellor House, relegating the civilians to a back room and finally to the cellar.

Hooker now had troops on Lee's front and rear and boasted that the enemy "must either ingloriously fly, or come out from behind his defenses and give us battle on our own ground, where certain destruction awaits him." Lee, having no intention of retreat, decided that Sedgwick was the lesser danger, left a small force to hold the Fredericksburg lines, and brought everybody else out to attack Hooker's turning column. On May 1, Lee struck Hooker moving leisurely toward Fredericksburg. The

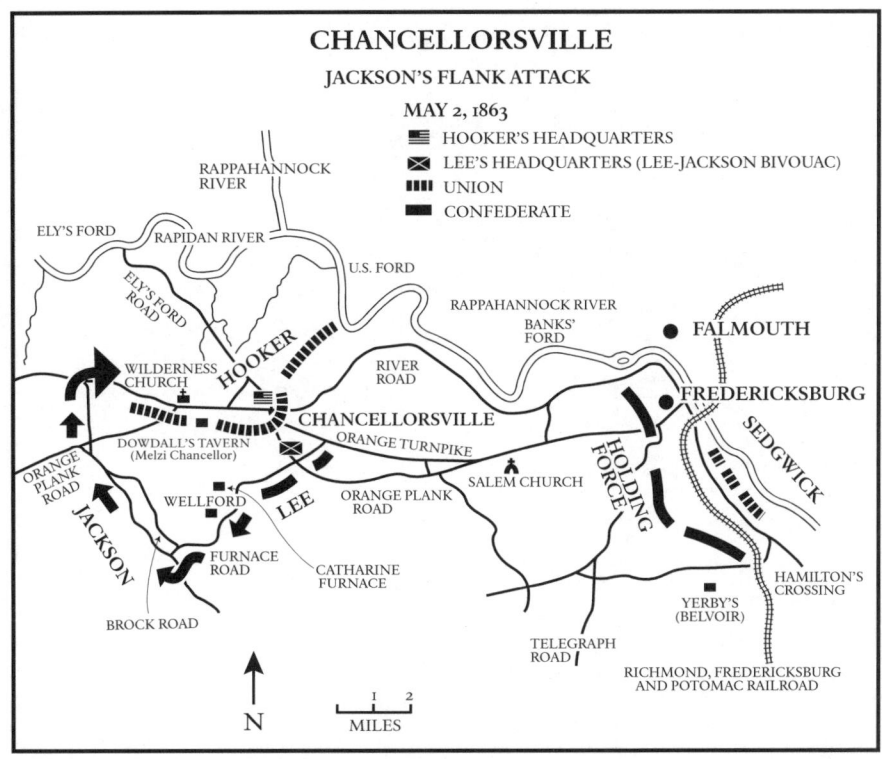

Confederates were courting the destruction Hooker promised. Taken aback, Hooker wondered whether Lee had been reinforced. (General Longstreet and two divisions were absent.) Hooker's confidence oozed. Relinquishing the offensive, he retreated to Chancellorsville and took up a defensive position.

The Confederates advanced and Lee sent out scouts and cavalry to study the Union lines. Word came back that the Union left and center were strong. Those positions were stronger even than the Confederates realized. The left rested on the Rappahannock below U.S. Ford. From the river, following the steep banks of a stream, the Yankee boys were rapidly throwing up earthworks to Chancellorsville; there the line curved and ran westward along the Orange Turnpike. The Confederate cavalry

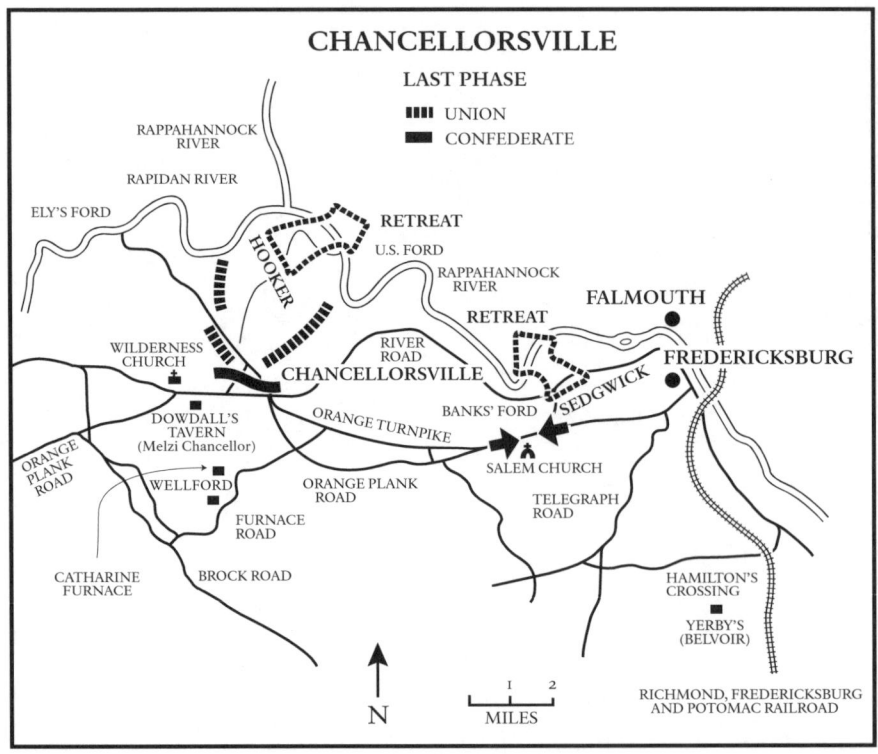

reported that the westward end, the right flank of Hooker's bow-shaped line, about three miles beyond Chancellorsville, seemed vulnerable. It simply came to an end without resting on any natural obstacle. The troops comprising that flank were sprawled in a large clearing, isolated by a section of woodland from the Chancellorsville clearing. Thus, Hooker's right flank, held by Oliver O. Howard's corps, became the target of Confederate plans.

Sitting around a little camp fire (the early May nights being chilly) at the junction of the Orange Plank Road and the Furnace Road, Lee and Jackson weighed possibilities. Cavalry could ride cross-country, but how might the infantry best reach Hooker's exposed right wing? The area was the eastern edge of a tangled second-growth forest called the Wilderness. Roads were few. Before the war, the main road to the mountains was the Orange Plank Road, which had absorbed in places the older Turnpike. Other than that dual system, all of it in poor repair, and a narrow north-south route called the Brock Road, the ways were local trails.

Chaplain Lacy knew the area. His brother's house Ellwood stood just a few miles west. He explained the topography to the generals. The road the Confederates were intrenched along, the Furnace Road, ran down to Wellford's iron works, the Catharine Furnace, a failed small industry reopened to produce pig iron for the Confederacy. From the Furnace a trail presumably meandered to the Brock Road. A flanking force could proceed northward on the Brock Road toward the Turnpike. Lacy did not remember all the ins and outs; young Charles Wellford would be a good guide.

Plans were made accordingly. Jackson would execute a flank movement. Guidance was secured, and the next morning Lee bade Jackson Godspeed. As Jackson's battle-stained veterans tramped down the Furnace Road, Lee remained in place with a token force to keep Hooker occupied. The marchers were spotted from Hazel Grove, a high point west of Chancellorsville, and Union troops attacked Jackson at the Furnace. The Union high command reasoned that the Confederates were finally retreating, as expected. Jackson's rear guard staved off the attack, while his column moved on. This mistaken Union emphasis further weakened Hooker's right flank. Though a few individuals in Howard's corps correctly interpreted Jackson's movement, nobody paid them any attention. When Jackson's columns reached the Brock Road, it turned south, away from the enemy, but soon thereafter reversed itself into a parallel woods road and then came out into the Brock Road and continued northward.

Reaching the Orange Turnpike during the late afternoon, the marchers turned right, deployed into battle lines and swept eastward in two-mile waves, washing destruction across the clearing where Howard's men had been contentedly preparing supper. Past the little Wilderness Baptist Church, past old Dowdall's Tavern, where General Howard vainly strove to stay the rout, the panic-stricken soldiers fled, through the woods to the east and on into the Chancellorsville clearing and beyond.

In the hurly-burly of battle, Jackson's grayjackets themselves became mixed and confused. They were halted to regroup; Ambrose Powell Hill's Division was ordered up from the rear. At the front, a side trail, the Bullock Road, entered the highway in the woods a mile west of Chancellorsville. General Jackson, staff members and couriers gathered around that junction. The general and a few attendants rode forward to reconnoiter. Meantime, at Chancellorsville Hooker busied himself in attempting to retrieve the situation. He sent fresh well-disciplined troops toward the west. Jackson's little cavalcade, on the point of running into those units, headed back to the Confederate lines. It was now about nine o'clock. Sporadic shots crackled through the woodland, the flare of muskets sparking like alien fireflies, larger than life.

Hill's men, taking over the front line along the Bullock Road were edgy. They did not intend to be caught by Federal counterattack; mounted figures were charging toward them. They met the situation with a volley. Powell Hill called to his men to cease firing. Joseph Morrison yelled that they were shooting at their own people. "It's a lie," came an answering scream, "Pour it into them, boys!" The boys complied. Jackson was caught by the next volley, once in the right hand, twice in the left arm. Little Sorrel bolted toward the enemy and Jackson had trouble facing him about. The corps signal officer, Captain R. E. Wilbourn, and another officer found their way to the general and helped him dismount. The other officer went off for assistance. After a while a cluster of people, including Hill, gathered around the fallen chief. Wilbourn made a tourniquet out of a handkerchief. Jackson somewhat reluctantly, accepted a sup of whiskey. Firing by both sides continued.

The wounded man was walked toward the rear until litter bearers arrived. The party then cautiously proceeded westward. Firing accelerated; Union cannon shot and Minié balls hailed down the road. One litter bearer was hit; another ran away. Smith and Morrison and Captain

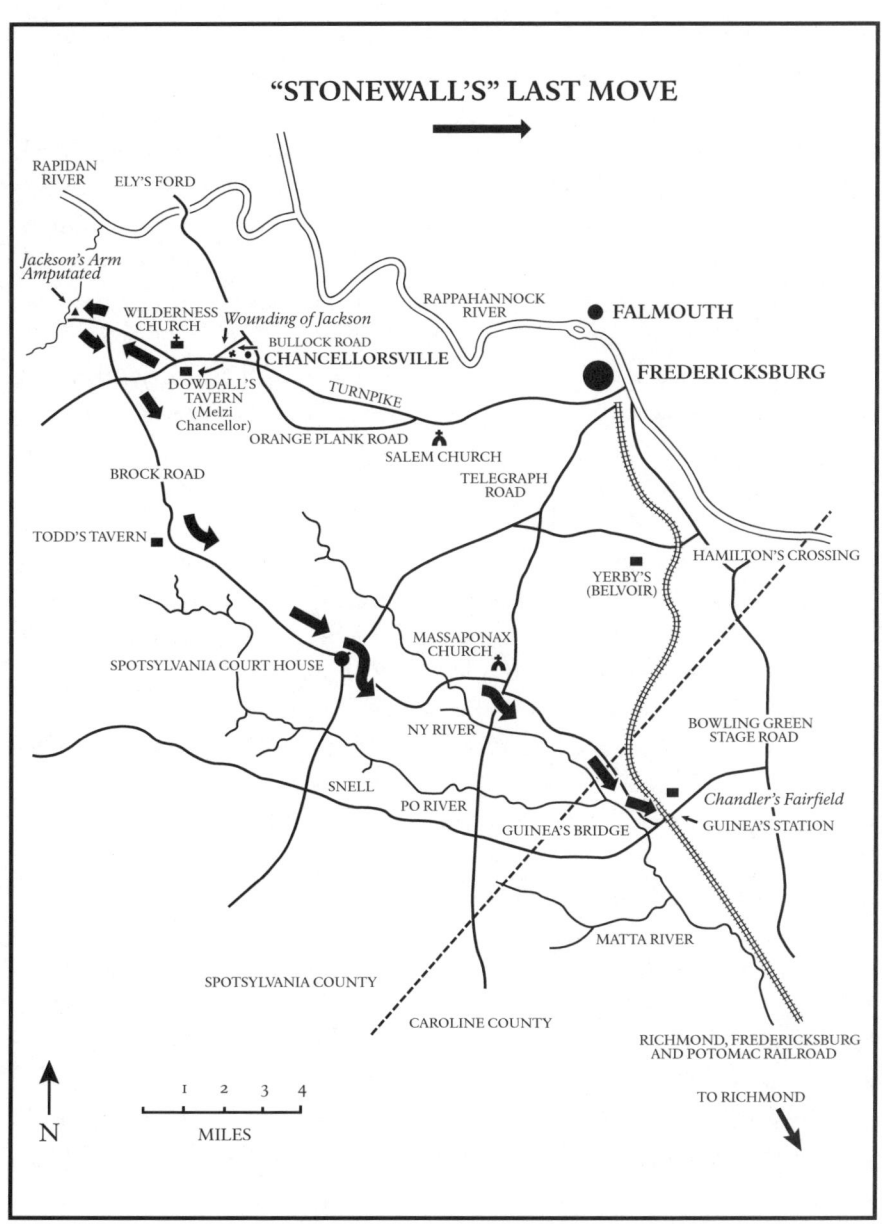

Benjamin Watkins Leigh of Hill's staff threw themselves on the ground around the general's supine form and kept him from rising during the worst of the fusillade. Jackson said he could walk, so the party started off again. He soon tired. The party was having trouble with its led horses. Soldiers were met in increasing numbers, but veered away until they learned the identity of the casualty. Then there were volunteers enough for the stretcher bearing. Again on the litter, Jackson was carried deeper within his lines. His ordeal, however, increased. A bearer tripped and the general crashed down on his wounded arm.

Once more the party resumed its way and finally found an ambulance. Taking a roundabout route, the ambulance reached Dowdall's Tavern, so recently headquarters of Federal General Howard. The former hostelry was the home of a member of the Chancellor clan, the Reverend Melzi Chancellor, a Baptist preacher. At Melzi's, Dr. Hunter McGuire, the corps medical director, greeted General Jackson with tactful solicitude. The handkerchief had slipped. Dr. McGuire stopped the renewed bleeding and gave the patient whiskey and morphia. Then began the three-mile ride to the field hospital overlooking Wilderness Run, next to the old Wilderness Tavern, another relic of by-gone stage-coach days.

The surgeon in charge had a tent in readiness. Jackson was given more whiskey and put under blankets. Well after midnight, Dr. McGuire told the patient they planned to administer chloroform and probe his wounds. Would it be all right to amputate if that seemed necessary? Jackson, the disciplinarian, himself ever obedient to constituted authority, told the doctor to proceed as seemed proper.

All the amenities then possible to a field hospital were at hand. Jackson had privacy, several doctors, and the balm of chloroform. Breathing in the anesthetic, he left his pain behind and murmured, "What an infinite blessing!"

Dr. McGuire first worked on the wound in the right hand, digging out a perfectly round ball (not a pointed Minié bullet), proof if any were

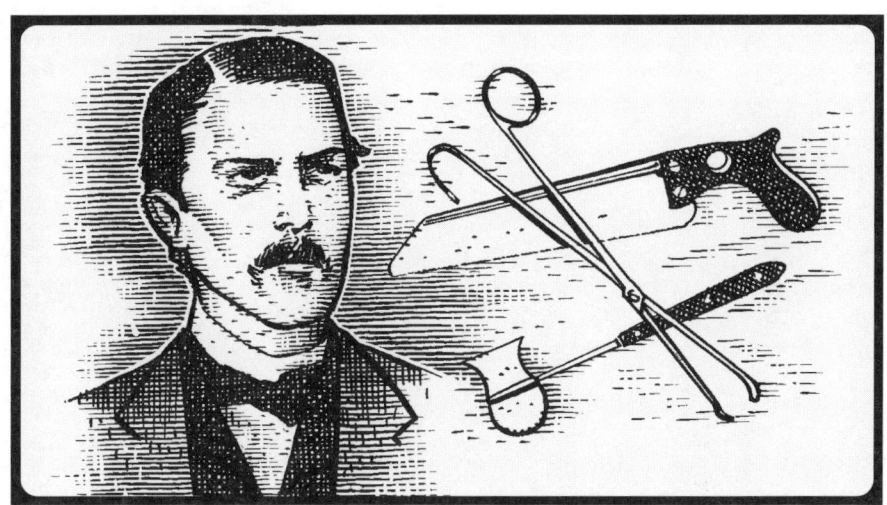

needed that Jackson had been shot by his own men. The Federals no longer used the smoothbore musket and its spherical projectile.

Investigation disclosed shattering of the bone in the upper left arm and severing of the main artery. Another bullet had ploughed its way through the lower arm. In those days gangrene followed such wounds. All agreed on the necessity of amputation. The doctors soon completed the routine operation and treated facial scratches inflicted by tree branches when Little Sorrel bolted.

Jackson came around nicely, took some coffee and seemed to rest comfortably. Later on he was told that Hill had been wounded soon after his own fall. Stuart the cavalryman exercised temporary command, but General Jackson could not cudgel his wits to send any advice. Just before his wounding, he planned a continuing strike, meaning for Hill to get between the enemy and U.S. Ford on the Rappahannock. The flank attack had already cut the Federals from the Rapidan. Now General Jackson's concern with those earthly rivers grew vague, and Deacon Jackson's soul, almost imperceptibly at first, began to seek another stream.

Destination Fairfield

As Sunday, May 3 wore on, Jackson brightened and was pleased to hear that the Federals had been driven from the Chancellorsville crossroads. He perked up enough to dictate a note telling Lee of his wounding and the transfer of command to Stuart.

In the afternoon James Power Smith read him Lee's answer. The commanding general regretted the price of a victory based on Jackson's skill and energy. "Could I have directed events, I should have chosen for the good of the country to be disabled in your stead." Jackson, touched, averred that the praise should go to God.

Then came another headquarters communication, an order for Dr. McGuire to accompany Jackson to a safer spot. Despite Confederate success, the campaign was not over. The enemy could conceivably reach the field hospital. Jackson felt no fear; he had always treated enemy wounded courteously and expected like treatment. He was ready to follow orders, however. When asked if he had any choice of destination, he recalled the kindness of the Chandlers at Guinea's Station. Their place might well be a good point, the doctors agreed. After Jackson improved he could be taken by rail to the outskirts of Richmond for a quiet convalescence near its facilities.

Early on May 4, his attendants placed the general in an army ambulance and set off down the Brock Road toward Spotsylvania Court House, first leg of the twenty-five mile journey to Thomas Coleman Chandler's Fairfield plantation. Topographical Engineer Jedediah Hotchkiss and a small body of pioneers rode ahead to clear the road. (Jackson had started the campaign with two engineers; young Keith Boswell fell dead in the mistaken firing which wounded the general.) Dr. McGuire took the vehicle in charge, with Chaplain Lacy and Aide-de-Camp Smith accompanying. The other aide, Joseph Morrison, had left for Richmond to stand by Anna. Meanwhile, the grapevine telegraph spread the news of Jackson's fall. Along the way country folk sympathetically watched the ambulance pass. At Spotsylvania Court House the party broke its journey by the village well, where the people gathered in awe and sorrow. From Spotsylvania the ambulance proceeded to Massaponax Church and on toward Guinea's Station through the holdings of Thomas Coleman Chandler's three older sons, William Samuel, Joseph Alsop, and Thomas Kay, whose adjoining lands in Spotsylvania and Caroline counties, abutted their father's Fairfield.

The boys got their properties from their grandfather, the late Samuel Alsop. His vast real estate holdings, slaves, livestock, equipment, and cash assets fully justified his nickname, "Rich Sam" Alsop.

Thomas Coleman Chandler owed his prosperity to Sam. He married Sam's daughter Clementina in 1825, received Alsop largesse, and lived successively on several Spotsylvania plantations. Clementina died in 1844. The next year Thomas, who loved to move about, purchased Fairfield, an old Thornton family place of 753½ acres, plus an additional 92 acres nearby, for $11,000 in hand paid, a substantial wad to plunk down in that day of hard money. (The home plot came out to a half acre because the Thornton graveyard, not subject to sale, occupied the other half.)

Thorntons had helped establish Caroline County, formed in 1727 and named for the wife of George II. The first Thornton to live in the Guinea area, Colonel Anthony Thornton of Ormsby, had been a member of the county Committee of Safety during the Revolution and a commander of the Caroline militia. His son John inherited the Fairfield land, bordering headwaters of the York. (Upstream from

nearby Guinea's Bridge, the little Po and Ny came together, and downstream the Matta joined to form the Mattapony.) John Thornton lived in his frame dwelling from the late 1700's onward. In 1828 he built a frame outbuilding, or "office," near the main house. Plantation offices often amounted to cottages, as did this one, an almost square story-and-a-half gable-roofed structure. In such outbuildings the business of the farm was transacted and the men of the family held convivial sway. Whatever the rights of a hunting dog in the big house, he always had the freedom of the office, amid the guns, fishing rods and sportive boys.

Just as John's father had provided for his family, so John acquired other lands and took care of his own children. The plantation system was faltering, however, and many Virginians sought their fortunes westward. Several Thorntons and neighbors struck out over the mountains. John hung on at Fairfield with his third wife Mildred until his death in 1844. He left the place to Mildred for life, after which it would be sold, the proceeds going to several children not yet endowed. When Mildred died the next year, Thomas Coleman Chandler purchased the estate from the executor.

Chandler acquired this place because of the adjoining Alsop property, to be inherited by his boys. Delighted in selling, he always bought again in the general area. He had no desire to leave Virginia for fresher fields. As fond of the married state as of the Old Dominion, he resolved to desert the single blessedness of his widowhood. A couple of years after buying Fairfield, the widower of fifty married Mary Elizabeth Frazer, twenty-eight.

Mr. Chandler disliked John Thornton's house. In the words of his daughter Lucy, spoken years later, he "did not care for" the antique frame building. He was an up-to-the-minute man with money to indulge himself, and he had, furthermore, quite a family to house. His eldest son William was already out of the home circle by 1850, but old Thomas still had Joseph, Thomas K., Mildred, Henry, Mary (all Clementina's children), and the second wife's James. Lucy was born in 1851; another daughter, Elizabeth, came along in 1853 and Nannie in 1855.

In 1854, between Elizabeth and Nannie, father Chandler moved everybody into the Thornton office, where they really were crowded, while the old house was torn down and a new one a-building. To make the temporary abode more convenient, he added a leanto and put three-quarter height shutters on the windows, protecting privacy while still admitting light.

(During this decade Joseph went to Philadelphia and graduated in medicine. He practiced in the Fairfield office before settling with a bride on his own land.)

Thomas Coleman Chandler's new brick dwelling rose plain and substantial, two floors and an attic over the half basement in which were kitchen and dining room. (At this period, Virginians were giving up year-round outdoor kitchens.) A large first-floor parlor with folding doors could be made into two rooms. From the first floor a spiral stairway led to the sleeping chambers. Two chimneys at each end of the rectangular gable-roofed structure allowed for ample heating. A long porch on the east side, or front, above basement level, faced the carriage drive.

Behind the house, three terraces followed the slope to the railroad. The first terrace was planted in flowers and shrubs, the second in grapes and other fruit, the third in vegetables. Down the center ran a walk and steps, flanked by mock orange and purple and white lilacs. Lily of the valley brightened May's shady corners after the yellow jonquils bloomed in the yard between dwelling and office.

Off one corner of the office, a pyramid-roofed meat house kept the family bacon and hams. Off the other office corner, a little upright structure, topping the stone-lined wall, housed the windlass that creaked up the wooden bucket of never-failing sweet water.

South of the office stood a small log barn or stable, and some distance beyond that the regular stables. Slave quarters and the ice house were north of the dwelling. In cold winters neighboring ponds furnished a plentitude of ice to pack deep in the pit, the sawdust-covered blocks ready to cool the lemonade of the summer.

The Chandlers enjoyed their new house on the verdant plateau of Fairfield, while talk of coming war shook Virginia, caught between the ambitions of the industrial North and the archaic economy of slavery and cotton. Still vigorous, old gentleman farmer Chandler, while nowhere near as rich as the Deep South grandees who fomented secession, maintained his position. On the eve of civil strife, the valley of the Mattapony dozed in the sun, the plantation houses along the ridges looking down on fields of corn and tobacco, melons and

cucumber vines. In 1860 Thomas Coleman Chandler and his three elder sons were taxed for over 2,500 acres of that countryside and 67 slaves of twelve years and up. Mr. Chandler himself possessed 38 slaves twelve years and up and 740 acres of land. (He had changed the acreage of his original Thornton purchase by selling and buying.) He owned a fair amount of livestock too, including 16 horses and 77 sheep and hogs.

Though the onset of war changed conditions and inflation gradually sapped the wealth of all, the Chandlers got on well enough, sharing their bounty with anyone less fortunate. The sons, moreover, disproved the total truth of the saying that it was a rich man's war and a poor man's fight. Henry, in his twenties, and William and Thomas K., in their thirties, served as privates in the Confederate cavalry.

Now, midway of the war, on Monday, May 4, 1863, as Jackson's ambulance rolled southeastward, the Fairfield household went about its accustomed courses. The children amused themselves around the place. Mrs. Chandler, in addition to her routine domestic work, was looking after several wounded Confederates, whom she nursed in the big house itself. Across the side yard, the once busy office stood empty, except for some old furniture and odds and ends stored there. On the edge of the activity, the little building looked lonely. Reflecting the shifting light of a chancy spring day, the Fairfield office loomed like a haunted house, uninhabited, waiting.

Over the River

That afternoon, Mrs. Chandler sat resting on the porch with twelve-year-old Lucy, a serious child often in her mother's company. Their desultory conversation was broken by a courier, dashing up to inform the household of the wounded Jackson's imminent arrival. Rising easily to the emergency, the chatelaine summoned two of her servants, Mammy Phyllis and Aunt Judy. The women searched out linens and prepared a bed in the parlor, a fitting place for the general, who should have stayed there during that cold weather last winter.

Then, riding ahead of the ambulance party, Chaplain Lacy arrived to make preliminary arrangements. He soon discovered the crowded condition of the dwelling. The chaplain considered the house too noisy and public for General Jackson's well-being. Mrs. Chandler assured him they would all be very quiet, but he remained unconvinced. Dr. McGuire, coming along soon afterward, agreed with Lacy, especially when he learned that a case or two of erysipelas had occurred there. Why not use the little house out in the yard? suggested the chaplain.

Mrs. Chandler and several servants got busy all over again, moving the bed to the office. The day had turned stormy. A chill hung in the air of the unused cottage. Quickly, the hostess and her helpers kindled fire. Then Mrs. Chandler and Lucy repaired to the second story of the big house to watch for the ambulance.

The business of war had affected Mr. Chandler's place somewhat. A rutted military road led from the railway past the end of the log shed, turning left toward the old carriage drive. As members of the family and servants, their voices hushed, looked on, the tired mules pulled the ambulance up the slope and followed the military party along a paling fence which separated the office yard from the front grounds. Thomas Coleman Chandler stood by the gate. The ambulance stopped and attendants removed the general. Mr. Chandler, giving wholehearted welcome, deplored the occasion of the visit. The general, his injured hand bandaged, apologized for not shaking hands.

Five months since, Mr. Chandler and Lucy had walked over to Jackson's tent near the slave quarters and offered use of their parlor. The general was not going into the parlor this time either, but he was finally to sleep under a roof at Fairfield.

Despite disuse, the office was in good repair. The walls had recently been whitewashed. Lucy ever after proudly remembered that her mother always kept it clean and "there was a wonderful view of our terraced garden, with its lovely flowers."

Through the little porch at the gable end the party bore Jackson into an entry. Ahead were two fairly spacious rooms, each with a fireplace. The bed had been put in the rightward of these, the one overlooking the gardens and railroad. He was quickly bedded down, warm and content.

The adjoining room lent itself nicely for a waiting room and a place to prepare medicines and roll bandages. A small room, cut off from the entry by a wooden partition, could, if necessary, hold baggage and gear. (Whatever the good housekeeping, family articles stored in various rooms gave a certain haphazard appearance.) A narrow stairway in the entry led steeply from Jackson's door to two half-story chambers. McGuire, Smith and other attendants would use the larger of these. The general's body servant Jim Lewis prepared to shake down in the other, facing the big house.

Mrs. Chandler's servants scurried about bringing over whatever would make the office more home-like, including a mantel clock for Jackson's room.

The general's martial ardor had revived during the day. He patiently endured the long rough journey, discussing Hooker's strategy and chatting about his old brigade, the bulwark of First Manassas. The brigade deserved the nickname "Stonewall," he asserted; he was only "Old Jack." By the time he reached Fairfield, about 8 p.m., he was ready for bed and soon fell asleep.

Before long, all were asleep, or, anyway, abed. Farmyard and household quieted, as the chant of the whippoorwills heralded darkness. Outside Jim's window, the delicate fronds of the locust trees quivered in the night wind.

The next morning, Tuesday, May 5, Dr. McGuire changed bandages. The wounds showed the first stage of healing. Mrs. Chandler had made the sick room quite habitable, adding a lounge and chairs to the furnishings. The bright chamber harbored no visible spectre of gloom. Jackson enjoyed his breakfast. Later on, Chaplain Lacy led morning prayers. You must come in every morning, Jackson told him, but for the rest of the time stay with the troops. (The general was committing the chaplain to a lot of riding.) Lacy officially was not a personal minister to Jackson. He was a Confederate chaplain. "I have always," said Jackson, "tried to set the troops a good example." Jed Hotchkiss also returned to the battlefront that day. James Power Smith remained with his chief, ready to fetch and carry or discuss military affairs or Holy Writ, all of which he did.

On a rainy May 6 Jackson and Smith contentedly continued their theological discourse. Not so happily engaged, Hooker's men huddled on the Union side of the Rappahannock, having retreated over U.S. Ford during the night.

(While Lee drove Hooker from the Chancellorsville crossroads on May 3, Sedgwick had broken the Confederate lines at Fredericksburg and prepared to march westward to Hooker's assistance. Lee, taking the chance that Hooker would not venture from his defences covering

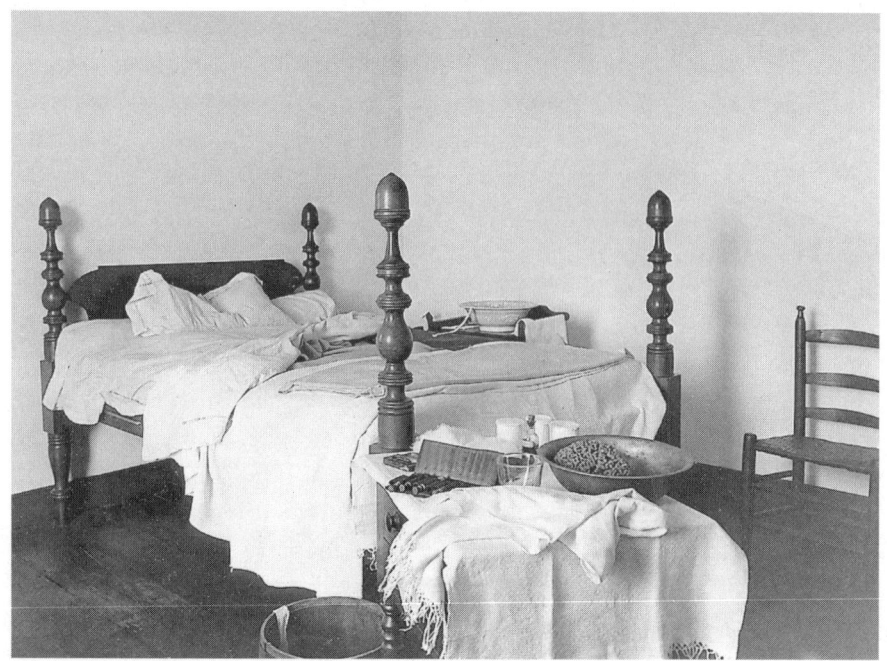
Original Jackson death bed and period furnishings.

U.S. Ford, left a few men to contain Hooker and doubled back to defeat Sedgwick at Salem Church. Sedgwick retreated over the nearby Rappahannock at Banks' Ford. Then Lee returned to Chancellorsville, only to find the outbluffed Hooker flown away.)

The bones of the Chancellor House stood in a ravaged landscape, victim of the South's own artillery. The Chancellor refugees, rescued by a Union staff officer, were temporary guests in Hooker's lines.

To Lee's tent on the battlefield Chaplain Lacy found his way Wednesday, May 6, reported on events at Fairfield, and requested permission to borrow Dr. Samuel B. Morrison, surgeon in one of Jackson's divisions. Morrison, Mrs. Jackson's kinsman, was the general's family physician. His presence would be reassuring. It would also allow

Jackson death room as restored during the 1960s. The mantel clock ticked away Jackson's ebbing life.

Dr. McGuire to get some sleep. (McGuire had been attending his patient day and night and made little use of the upstairs room.)

Lacy carried to Fairfield promise of Dr. Morrison and Lee's affectionate regards to Jackson: ". . . tell him to make haste and get well, and come back to me as soon as he can. He has lost his left arm; but I have lost my right arm."

That night Hunter McGuire could stay awake no longer. He instructed Jim to keep vigil and collapsed on the lounge in the sick room. During the early hours of May 7 the General's stomach became queasy. The believer in quaint therapies favored application of a wet towel and told Jim to apply one. Dr. McGuire had indulged a similar whim on the journey down. Under these particular circumstances, the doctor asleep and all, Jim did not think much of the idea. Jackson ordered him to do as bid and not to wake up McGuire. Jim reluctantly obeyed. Something more than nausea, however, pervaded Jackson's system. Increasing pain surged through his side. At dawn, he told Jim to awaken the doctor.

McGuire recognized the onset of pneumonia. (Despite the beliefs of the time, the wet towel did not cause the disease, which, already present, was the unseen spectre in that sick room.) Jackson now faced a redoubtable antagonist, hard to outflank.

Mrs. Jackson was on her way to help her husband in his fight. Aware of the wounding since Sunday, Anna had been unable to reach him sooner because of Hooker's cavalry. A raid led by General George Stoneman, accomplishing little else, temporarily disrupted rail service and unsettled the countryside above Richmond. Joseph Morrison did not manage to get through until Tuesday. On Thursday, May 7, brother and sister, Nurse Hetty and baby Julia rode up in an armed train.

The General was doing "pretty well," his wife was told. She could not see him just yet, the doctor was dressing his wounds. Anna sensed trouble. Mrs. Chandler took in the little family tenderly and went to prepare upstairs quarters in the big house. While walking off her nervousness on the porch, the distraught Anna saw a body being dug up. She learned it was that of General Frank Paxton, commander of Jackson's old brigade, temporarily interred here after his death at Chancellorsville. A Lexington friend and neighbor! This was a chilling introduction to Fairfield.

Once in the sick room, she somewhat mastered show of emotion, but not her apprehension. Unlike her husband, she could not say, "Never take counsel of your fears." There he lay now, how different from the cavalier of Yerby's, the sunny *esposo* of hardly more than a week ago! His appearance wrung her heart. In anguish she counted the labored breaths and despaired over the stupor that set him apart.

Between bouts of morphia-induced drowsiness, Jackson expressed appreciation of her presence. Once he rallied enough to admonish her to cheer up and not pull such a long face. Several times he expressed his love and asked her to pray for him. He wanted the baby brought in, he said, directly he felt better. Every now and then the battlefield obtruded and he came out with fragmentary orders.

Opiates eased pain. Dr. McGuire also cupped. Cupping, the application of heated glass cups to the chest, pulled blood into the area. Dr. Samuel Morrison arrived in the afternoon. Though he bore no magic potions, at least his presence forced a glow of recognition in the sunken eyes. Jackson smiled and said: "That's an old, familiar face." The two doctors decided to send Smith for Dr. David Tucker, a Richmond specialist. Smith was also to bring back Mrs. Moses D. Hoge, the minister's wife in whose home Anna had been staying. Mrs. Hoge would help with the baby while Anna devoted full time to her husband.

Dr. Tucker it developed, could not come up right away. Meanwhile, two other physicians suggested by McGuire arrived for consultation. The condition of the wounds gratified everybody. As to the pneumonia, all they could do was cup and blister, the hot plaster adding new pain, treatment never reaching the hidden enemy, the unknown germ within.

All through May 8 Jackson clutched at his eager soul. He would not let it slip away yet. He was unafraid and ready to abide by Heavenly will. "But," he said to Dr. Morrison, "I do not believe that I shall die at this time; I am persuaded the Almighty has yet a work for me to perform."

On Saturday, May 9, Dr. Tucker arrived. (The Chandlers were feeding about as many doctors as patients in their combined Fairfield hospitals, big house and office.) Though weaker than ever, Jackson had moments of insight. He remarked to Dr. McGuire, "I see from the number of physicians that you think my condition dangerous, but I thank God, if it is His will, that I am ready to go."

He asked for the baby and lightly touched her with his splinted hand. Time dragged on. Outside, spring sunlight quickened the world of nature. It was a day to breathe deep. In the office, fluid filled the lungs of Jackson and he could scarcely breathe at all. He could, however, muster strength to call for Lacy and to question the chaplain about church attendance in the camps. Furthermore, Lacy must preach to the soldiers tomorrow, not remain at Guinea's for the general's sake.

Drugged and drowsy, Jackson often dozed. His mind came and went. He thought himself again on the battlefield: "Order A. P. Hill to prepare for action . . . Pass the infantry to the front." Anna suggested he might like to hear some passage from the Bible. He failed to pay attention to her reading. Then Anna and Joseph sang for him, Watts' hymn of the Fifty-first Psalm, beginning:

> *Shew pity, Lord; O Lord, forgive;*
> *Let a repenting rebel live;*
> *Are not thy mercies large and free?*
> *May not a sinner trust in thee?*

The singing soothed him, and the irony of the second line seemed lost on all; as far as the Civil War was concerned, he remained a Rebel unrepentant.

"I think I will be better by morning," said the general.

Again and again, Deacon Jackson had expressed faith in God's will, but the hardy soldier kept believing he would live to man once more the ramparts of Rappahannock and Rapidan. The soul, all the while, sought the main stream of its choice.

On Sunday, May 10, both Anna and Dr. McGuire warned the patient that his end approached. He seemed reconciled and, smiling, whispered endearments to Julia, whom Mrs. Hoge had brought over for a farewell visit. Then, lapsing into unconsciousness, he appeared as one already dead. He aroused, however, to greet young Alexander

Pendleton, a favorite staff officer. Lacy was preaching at headquarters today, reported "Sandie," and the whole army prayed for the General's recovery.

"They are very kind . . ." replied Jackson, and, after a pause: "It is the Lord's Day . . . My wish is fulfilled. I have always desired to die on Sunday."

He refused brandy offered by McGuire and slipped into delirium. A jumble of words, distinct and indistinct, domestic and military, passed out his thin dry lips.

On the mantel the Chandler clock had hour by hour struck away the time, its resounding bongs, startling from so small a mechanism, filling the room. Now it was ticking off the minutes. At three fifteen of a lovely day, Thomas Jackson's soul reached out: "Let us cross over the river, and rest under the shade of the trees."

Except when preparing food for the sick room, Mrs. Chandler, Lucy at her heels, spent her daylight hours watching the office. In the last days, even Lucy knew no hope was held for the general's recovery. She wished she could die in his place, because then only her family would be sorry, "but if General Jackson dies, everybody will be sorry." Lucy and her mother realized that the general had died when they saw his wife leaving the office, supported by Smith and Joseph Morrison.

The news was telegraphed to Richmond.

His attendants shrouded him in a dark civilian suit, since the General's uniform was blood-stained and cut. Over the suit they wrapped a blue military overcoat. This they did in the office. An open wooden coffin held the mortal remains of "Stonewall" Jackson. Sunday night, however, a company of embalmers, sent by the governor of Virginia, arrived from Richmond with a metallic coffin. These men further prepared the body.

The metallic coffin was placed in the Chandler parlor, where Jackson at long last accepted the hospitality of the big house.

The next day householders and staff gathered flowers in simple tribute to a dead friend. Lucy herself picked a special bunch. "Oh, how willingly I would have died for him," cried the child.

Anna Jackson gazed on the face swathed in lily of the valley, the flower of humility, snow-white and sweet smelling. She would never again see that plant without recalling the scene.

Later in the day, the casket was borne down the walk over the terraces to the railroad. A separate car of the Richmond train was reserved for Mrs. Jackson and party, which included Mr. and Mrs. Chandler.

The little engine steamed off down the track, pulling behind it the fallen champion. In April, Thomas had warmly welcomed Anna at Guinea's Station. In May, cold and eternally secretive, the mythic Lieutenant General T. J. Jackson, aged 39, left Guinea's with his widow. His obsequies would be impressive, while the whole South mourned. There would be parading and services and lying in state in Mr. Jefferson's classic capitol. At Lexington, the honors would begin again, ending May 15 with a funeral in the Presbyterian church and burial in the town cemetery, not far from the battlements of V.M.I., where the obscure Major Jackson, an uninspiring teacher, had been the butt of cadet jokes.

A Busy Depot

Guinea's was a railroad station long before Jackson ever saw the place, and the name predated the station. During the early eighteenth century, Michael Guiney kept a tavern at the crossing of the Po-Ny, on the recent hunting ground of the native red man. The Guiney family died out, but not the name, firmly attached to the bridge and area. (Pronounced with the short *i*, like the African fowl, the word was corrupted to *Guinea*.) When the railroad from Richmond reached the vicinity about a hundred years after the tavern keeper's death, the station established near the bridge also acquired his name.

The Civil War found Guinea's a sleepy rural stop. Though on the line to the Confederacy's northern frontier, the station saw no great commotion during the first months of conflict. The enemy reached the area in May of 1862 but hardly disturbed the quietude. "No more pleasing region for campaigning purposes ever came in my line of march," wrote one of the invaders. "The roads are good, water plenty, and there are farms enough for foraging purposes and fences enough for fuel. If the soldier asks for anything besides these requisites he has pleasing landscapes, extensive views, and houses planned on a grand scale . . ."

This soldier was part of a reconnaissance probing out from Fredericksburg, just occupied by Irvin McDowell. In George B. McClellan's campaign against Richmond, McDowell was scheduled to descend southward while McClellan sailed down Chesapeake Bay and then marched westward up the Peninsula between the James and York rivers.

The little advanced group stayed around Guinea only five days, and McDowell's force soon left the Fredericksburg area. "Stonewall"

Jackson's Shenandoah Valley Campaign frightened the Washington authorities, disrupting Union plans. McDowell was pulled back, leaving only a detachment at Fredericksburg. Meanwhile, Jackson joined Lee at Richmond to push McClellan down the Peninsula.

The Federals completely evacuated the Fredericksburg area in late summer. Lee's victory of Second Manassas caused all Federal units to seek the safety of the Washington forts. The Confederates then elected to hold the line of the Rappahannock, halfway between the capitals, and stopped Burnside when he tried to come through Fredericksburg. That time the Union occupation of the old town was brief and costly.

Since the section of railroad from Fredericksburg five miles down to a crossing called Hamilton's lay open to Federal long-range cannon across the Rappahannock, Lee had destroyed the track. A military railhead grew up around Hamilton's Crossing, but Guinea's Station, seven miles farther south, became the main base. Troops going and coming tented and bivouacked round about, and quartermaster soldiers labored to load the wagons supplying Lee's widely scattered encampments. From camp and battlefield, sick and wounded boarded the cars to Richmond.

The Guinea neighborhood more and more felt the heel of Mars, whose votaries, whether foe or friend, appreciated a region of "farms enough for foraging purposes and fences enough for fuel." Suffering no real devastation, everybody thereabouts nevertheless fully realized a war was going on.

The brief December sojourn of Jackson's Corps at Fairfield must have impinged on rail fences, despite Jackson's habit of discouraging depredation. That attitude and his refusal of indoor hospitality (a rule he sometimes broke) stemmed from deep convictions.

The convictions of the jovial cavalryman Fitzhugh Lee never precluded shelter. After the Battle of Fredericksburg, being in the Guinea neighborhood, he settled comfortably in the Chandler office, all ready for Christmas. "Jeb" Stuart interrupted holiday plans, however, by

ordering him off to raid across the Rappahannock on Christmas Eve. Returned again with gay stories for the young Chandlers, "Fitz" Lee did not stay at Guinea's long. His brigade left in February and assumed picket duty along the upper Rappahannock. The office reverted to echoing playrooms for the children.

Guinea's was busier than ever during and after the Chancellorsville Campaign, and the Fairfield office, touched with fame by the death of Jackson, saw further hospital use. In the weeks following Chancellorsville, sickness hit many who had escaped bullets. One sufferer, "Sandie" Pendleton, was nursed back to health by Mrs. Chandler in the same room and on the same bed where General Jackson had died. He recovered to survive Gettysburg, but he did not outlive the war.

Then came a period of returning quiet for Guinea's Station and Fairfield, while George Gordon Meade, Hooker's successor, defeated Lee at Gettysburg, where Jackson's absence was first keenly felt.

The next spring, 1864, Ulysses S. Grant, newly appointed chief of all the Union armies, joined Meade. Grant set out to conquer Lee and vowed he would take no backward step. Leaving the deadly forest and fields of the Wilderness and Spotsylvania, Grant pushed on toward Richmond. Guinea's was about to see the enemy again, and in far greater numbers than the reconnoiterers of 1862.

From Spotsylvania Lee fell back to contest Grant's use of the main Richmond road, thus forcing detours for Union marchers. Early on May 21, Union troops passing Guinea's Station had a brush with Confederates. Getting word of this, Meade, who regarded Guinea's Bridge as a potential danger to his flanks, ordered those units to backtrack and halt around Guinea's. Other troops were then directed toward that point. (All the Federals ultimately passed through Guinea's Station.)

In the meantime, as Grant and Meade themselves came riding down part of the route followed by Jackson's ambulance the year

Chandler office in decay about 1880.

Chandler office, smokehouse and crumbling main dwelling early twentieth century.

From a photograph in the possession of Fredericksburg National Military park.

Chandler office and main dwelling, late nineteenth century dilapidation.

From "A History of Caroline County, Virginia" by Marshall Wingfield.

before, Confederate cavalry at Guinea's Bridge stepped up demonstrations. Arriving at Guinea's, Grant and Meade and their staffs found their wagon train somewhat alone. The troops passing through had not yet got back to halt there, and the others were not yet up. Meade's urbane aide, the Bostonian Theodore Lyman, wrote to his wife that the quartermaster was "looking very blank." Grizzled Marsena R. Patrick, the provost marshal, noted in his diary that "quite an alarm" ensued. Headquarters troops, however, soon pushed the Ninth and other Virginia cavalry regiments back over the bridge, with slight loss to either side.

A Union regimental historian, writing forty years after the event, daubed a picture which Grant and Meade might not have recognized. According to that account, dashing Yankee cavalry and gaily uniformed infantry in a story-book charge chased the Rebels back to and over the bridge, under the eyes of Grant and Meade, who perched on the railway station fence and cooly smoked their cigars.

Almost caught out, headquarters may not really have been in great danger, but the affair gained some notoriety around the campfires as "the wagon train battle."

That evening, headquarters (Grant and Meade always stayed side by side) settled on the grounds of the Edmund S. Motley place, overlooking Fairfield. Lyman described Motley's as "a good house, with a store of fruit trees and rose bushes in flower." The strawberries were beginning to ripen, he wrote. "Old Motley was an elderly man of a certain sour dignity; a bitter rebel plainly" who pointed out to his guests the place where Jackson died.

General Grant, usually refraining from entering houses, liked to sit on plantation porches. When he dropped cigar ashes on Motley's porch, Mr. Motley admonished him for employing a roundabout way of burning the house. Perhaps to get away from the grim presence, Grant and his aide Horace Porter took a walk over to Fairfield and sat on that porch.

In a little while Mrs. Chandler came out. The officers rose, swept off their hats, and bowed. Mrs. Chandler, amazed at finding the Yankee chieftain, was not at all abashed and chatted with her callers as though they were neighbors who had dropped by. The easy, pleasant address of the Virginia gentlewoman charmed Grant and Porter. They found her sprightly conversation most entertaining. Then she mentioned the sadness over Fairfield, telling how Jackson, "of blessed memory," had been brought there after his wounding.

Grant remarked that he and Jackson, a fellow veteran of the Mexican War, had been together a year at West Point. He remembered Jackson as a sterling cadet, respected by all. "He was a gallant soldier and a Christian gentleman," said Grant, "and I can understand fully the admiration your people have for him."

Mrs. Chandler went on to talk of Jackson's pneumonia, blaming the wet applications. Coming to the Sunday when "he was taken from us," her voice broke. She could scarcely continue.

Grant bade a polite goodby and promised Mrs. Chandler he would have a guard placed over Fairfield to make sure no wandering soldiers damaged anything. Then he and Porter strolled back through the fields to their tents and supper.

They were among the first of the many tourists who have visited "Stonewall" Jackson's place of death.

Grant apparently missed another possible tourist attraction, Braddock's coach, which relic of the luckless British general reposed at "Guinness" Station, according to a note in *Harper's Weekly* later that summer. Grant really had little time for sightseeing. Guinea's was only a brief stop on this more fortunate warrior's progress. His tread was firm for Appomattox, albeit that name as yet meant nothing to him.

The Guinea area saw the last of the war when part of Sherman's army, behaving decorously, came through on the way to the Washington victory parade after the collapse of the Confederacy in the spring of 1865.

Fairfield: Decay and Restoration

Before the war ended, Thomas Coleman Chandler grew restless. He had not moved for almost twenty years. In December of 1863 he sold Fairfield to Dr. Edgar McKenney, having already purchased from Colonel Buckner White a neighboring establishment called Lake Farm.

Grant and Porter, however, found the Chandlers still at Fairfield in 1864. Indeed, Chandler paid taxes on it through 1865, and the conveyance to McKenney was not acknowledged by the signatures of Thomas C. and Mary Chandler until March 4, 1865.

About the time of the sale of Fairfield, Mrs. Chandler was reputed to have been very nervous, sometimes close to a breakdown. It has been thought that the projected move was for her benefit, to get her away from the scene of "Stonewall" Jackson's death. But she would not be far removed from that scene. Furthermore, the deed of Chandler's purchase of Lake Farm, dated April 29, 1863, was recorded the same day, before ever Jackson fell wounded. Mary Chandler may have suffered fits of the vapors, incidental to her age, but their connection with moving from Fairfield can be misconstrued. Her husband had a history of acquiring and disposing. It is rather likely that, fond of Fairfield, regardless of sad associations, she balked at leaving. She had been unable to prevent the purchase of Lake Farm, but she could stop, or at least delay, the transfer of Fairfield by withholding her signature.

Within five years of that move, Thomas Coleman Chandler decided to move again. He sold Lake Farm in April of 1869. (His wife did not get around to acknowledging that deed for over a year.) In May of 1869 he purchased part of a tract called Spring Hill, whereon he built a house he named Ingleside, less than three miles from Fairfield. In his seventies, he expected to be around a while yet.

Mary Frazer Chandler died in 1881, aged 62. That December, Thomas executed his last deed. He gave all livestock (then only "a few old Mules & one horse and a few head of Cattle"), farm implements, furniture, and farm of about 200 acres to his son James Goss Chandler. In exchange, James agreed to support Thomas and the family remaining at home, including an unmarried daughter, and to pay taxes.

Thomas Coleman Chandler, born 1798, died in 1890, the man of property now without any, but well off in comfort until the end.

Meantime, Fairfield was not prospering. After Dr. McKenney's death in the early 1870's, his widow began selling off land. By the turn of the century, the estate had become divided and run down, having passed through various hands. The old Thornton graveyard was lost. (That may have disappeared during Confederate occupation.) Tenants took little care of the buildings, and fire gutted the dwelling. Month by month, the once substantial brick house deteriorated. The office, too, suffered change and blight.

Memories of old Fairfield lingered in some hearts. The Reverend James Power Smith, for one, would never forget what happened there. Ordained after the war, he served the Fredericksburg Presbyterian Church before accepting an administrative post in Richmond. During the first week of August, 1903, he supervised erection of several granite historical markers around Fredericksburg. One at Fairfield noted the death of Jackson. This beginning of memorialization did not, unfortunately, halt decay.

The condition of Fairfield particularly distressed William H. White, an admirer of Jackson and an alumnus of the Virginia Military Institute who had fought as a cadet at New Market and instructed at V.M.I. after the war. He was president of the Richmond, Fredericksburg and Potomac Railroad in 1909. That year, hearing that Fairfield might be further cut up and lost, Mr. White bought five acres, including the houses. He transferred the property to the Railroad in 1911. (He later purchased some seven more acres, which his heirs turned over to the Railroad.)

At last, the place was under protection. Preservation of the office began immediately, but it was not deemed necessary to save the big house; so that was torn down.

As early as 1907, railroad literature mentioned that the place where "Stonewall" Jackson died could be seen from the train. Conductors would point out the office and give little talks to the passengers. Smith's marker, though near the railroad then, could not be read from passing trains, but, after acquisition by the Railroad, a large earthen ramp with letters in boxwood against a background of white gravel readily informed the travelers: "In this house Stonewall Jackson died, May 10, 1863."

A trickle of visitors left the trains to get a closer look. After World War I, the automobile brought more. In 1919, the Railroad placed a track walker there as caretaker. For some time, he continued to walk track in addition to keeping up the house and grounds. The house still had no furnishings.

Stark and bare, it nonetheless impressed a hardbitten British statesman, "That old house witnessed the downfall of the Southern Confederacy," exclaimed David Lloyd George, standing by the Fairfield office, Sunday, October 28, 1923. He had boarded his special train an hour earlier than scheduled in order to squeeze in a stop at Guinea's. His remark extended a statement made earlier in Fredericksburg: "No doubt the history of America would have to be rewritten had 'Stonewall' Jackson lived."

During the 1920's certain people wanted more done with the Fairfield office. A group of ladies, prodding the railroad people, began a campaign to bring about rehabilitation and furnishing. On Monday, November 15, 1926, these activists paid a publicized visit to Guinea and worked on the room where Jackson died, putting in simple

Restored Chandler office, showing lean-to. Main house stood to right.

furnishings and sprucing things up generally. One of the party, Mrs. Charles K. Pendleton, the former Lucy Chandler, told of Jackson's death and recalled the Fairfield of old. A woman reporter wrote that this day's activities constituted the beginnings of a Jackson museum. Although the office had been open to the public for some time, she noted, it was not until then "that it really became a shrine." She called it the Jackson Shrine, a name which has stuck with the house museum ever since.

In 1927, R. F. & P. President Eppa P. Hunton Jr., gave the word to have the Chandler office further repaired. Work was completed by the next spring, and the Railroad dedicated the Jackson Shrine, Friday, October 12, 1928, before a crowd of several hundred people, including Mrs. Lucy Chandler Pendleton and Dr. Stuart McGuire, son of Jackson's medical director Hunter McGuire.

After rehabilitation, the visitor could see there the bed on which Jackson died (formerly in the custody of Richmond's Confederate Museum); a piece of the blanket that had covered the general, donated by Mr. Chandler's great grandchildren, Florence, George and Henry Washington, of Caroline County, and the mantel clock which ticked away "Stonewall's" last days, presented by Lucy Chandler Pendleton of Ashland, Virginia.

In 1936, the Richmond, Fredericksburg and Potomac Railroad donated the Jackson Shrine and nine acres of land to the National Park Service to be a part of the Fredericksburg and Spotsylvania National Military Park.

In the 1960's, the National Park Service made a thoroughgoing historical restoration and furnished the building fully. Despite the years of decay and change, much original woodwork remains. The worn stairway James Power Smith, Jim Lewis and other attendants wearily ascended still rises to the very same floor where they walked softly. Though the downstairs floor rotted away, the flooring in Jackson's room is original—with the exception of three boards next to the southwest wall. Jackson's bed stands on antique Chandler boards, coming from Nyland, Joseph Chandler's abandoned house. Joseph, if he were to revisit the office, could look out his old wavy window panes, also from Nyland. Thus did restoration weave the strands of family history through decay and rebirth.

The clock on the mantel and the bed in the Jackson room have been augmented by period furniture. A lounge, such as the one whereon Dr. McGuire napped, stands in a corner. Medicines, basins and bandages on old tables and the apparent remnants of Jackson's last meal help recreate the scene of that fateful May week. An open Bible lies on an upholstered chair, as though Mrs. Jackson had left it there. Looking at the empty bed, made up in period sheets and pillows, we imagine that the General has just been removed.

Other rooms are furnished according to their use during the Jackson occupancy. We see furniture of the type the Chandlers brought over to make the party comfortable. Scattered throughout also are articles similar to the things the family had stored there. In the waiting room next to Jackson's chamber, Dr. Joseph Chandler's earlier use of the office is represented by a bookcase, presumably borrowed from the big house and not taken back when Joseph moved to his own place.

Evoking the past, the Chandler office mutely reminds us that man and his works rise up, flourish and are cut down. Less than a hundred and fifty years after Michael Guiney's tavern brawlers displaced the aborigines of the Mattapony, the doomed Thornton and Chandler plantation economy fell to the storm of war. The fate of Fairfield mirrors the postwar South. If the Confederacy died with Jackson in the Fairfield office, a way of life also expired in "that old house."

To the admirers of "Stonewall" Jackson, Lee's surrender at Appomattox was epilogue.

Acknowledgements

Among many kind persons assisting in the research which incidentally resulted in this booklet were: Mr. George H. S. King, Fredericksburg genealogist; the late Mr. T. Elliot Campbell, Caroline County Clerk; Mr. Cary Crismond, Spotsylvania County Clerk; the late Dr. C. H. Quenzel, librarian, and Miss Marguerite Carder, reference librarian, Mary Washington College, Fredericksburg; Mr. John W. Dudley of the Virginia State Library, Richmond; Mr. David C. Mearns, Library of Congress, Washington; Mr. John D. Cushing, librarian, Massachusetts Historical Society, Boston; the staff of the Fredericksburg Free Lance-Star; Dr. David S. Sparks, University of Maryland; Mr. C. E. Mervine Jr., assistant to the president, Richmond, Fredericksburg and Potomac Railroad; Dr. Henry J. Warthen, Richmond, Va; Mr. H. E. Thomas of Fredericksburg; Mr. Lee Wallace, National Park Service historian; Mr. Orville Carroll, N.P.S. architect; and the following Chandler descendants: Mrs. Henry Rose Carter of Ashland (daughter of Mrs. Lucy Chandler Pendleton); Mrs. Vernon D. Lucy Jr. (the former Florence Washington) of Guinea; and the late Mrs. Campbell Chandler of Guinea.